THE *FORWARD* Planner

Copyright © 2024 by Regina Burden & The Jamar Group
All rights reserved. This book or any portion thereof may not be reproduced or used in any manner whatsoever without the express written permission of the publisher except for the use of brief quotations in a book review.

Limits of Liability and Disclaimer of Warranty
The author and publisher shall not be liable for your misuse of this material. This book is strictly for informational purposes. The purpose of this book is to educate and entertain. The author and publisher do not guarantee anyone following these techniques, suggestions, tips, ideas, or strategies will become successful. The author and publisher shall have neither liability nor responsibility to anyone with respect to any loss or damage caused, or alleged to be caused, directly or indirectly by the information contained in this book. Views expressed in this publication do not necessarily reflect the views of the publisher.
Author Contact: thejamargroup@gmail.com

Printed in the United States of America
Keen Vision Publishing, LLC
www.publishwithkvp.com
ISBN: 978-1-955316-44-6

THIS PERSON IS MOVING **FORWARD**:

WELCOME TO THE *FORWARD* PLANNER!

Where Faith Meets Purpose and Your Dreams Take Off With Divine Guidance

Growing up, my parents ensured my siblings and I had a solid foundation in faith. It has been a priceless gift, a steady anchor in the stormy seas of life. Being raised in a faith-filled home and surrounded by friends who are believers taught me how to handle life's ups and downs. I found comfort and strength in knowing that divine love was always there for me, guiding me through life's twists and turns.

Since the beginning of my journey, faith has been like a guiding voice in my heart, shaping my beliefs, values, and dreams. Inside *The Forward Planner*, you will discover more than just tools to help you organize your time and tasks. Before you dig into planning, assess and dream about your desired life. *The Forward Planner* contains questions to spark your thoughts and nourish your spirit. Grounded in the timeless principle of faith, this planner is like a map for your journey—a journey toward purpose, fulfillment, and transformation. *The Forward Planner* is your opportunity to release your fears, embrace your flaws, and forgive yourself for past mistakes.

Life can feel overwhelming and directionless. Allow *The Forward Planner* to be your companion and accountability partner as you strive to stay focused. This planner is not just a tool to manage your schedule; it's a sanctuary for your soul, a daily reminder of the power of faith and intentionality in shaping your future.

So, let's journey together—hand in hand, heart in heart—toward a future filled with hope and possibility. I hope you will find the courage to chase your dreams with unwavering faith. Remember, no two journeys are the same. Allow the story of YOUR life to unfold within the pages of *The Forward Planner*, knowing that all things are possible with the guiding light of FAITH.

Regina Burden

Developer of The Forward Planner & Owner of the Jamar Group

FLAWS failure

friends focus

faith

fear family

THE FORWARD LIFE WHEEL

If used properly, these 8 f- words can help you move your life forward! Pull out your coloring utensils, and start your FORWARD plan with this short assessment. **On a scale of 1-9, how well are you using these f- words to propel you forward in life?** Color the space from one, all the way to the number that fits your rating. When you are done, consider this question: If you had a car with four wheels like your F- Wheel, how much moving forward would you do? What areas could use some work?

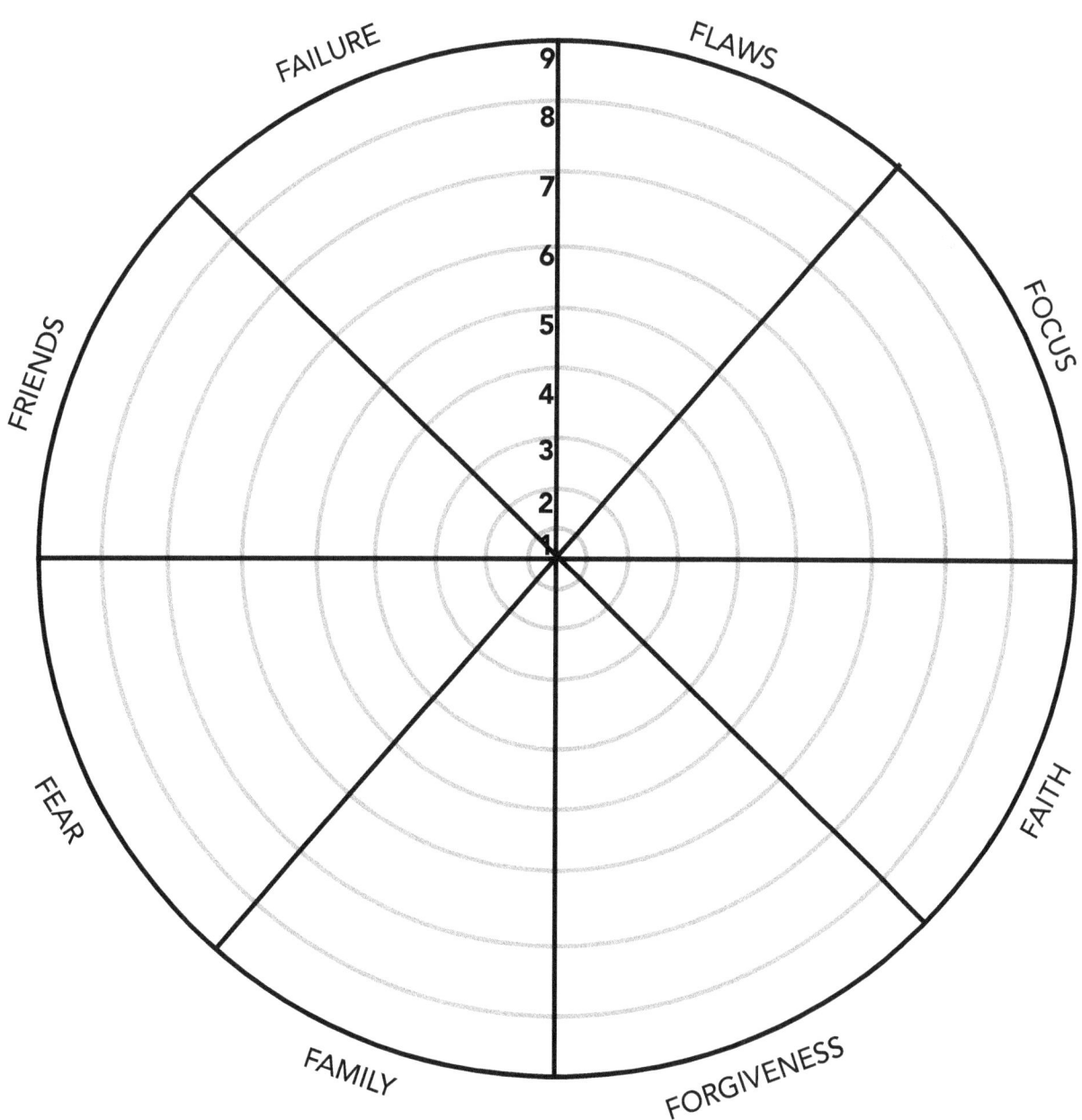

REFLECT & ASSESS

How did you feel about your life wheel results? Chances are, there are a few areas that may need a little work. Answer the next questions about your failures, flaws, focus, faith, forgiveness, friends, fear, and family, before you begin planning. These questions are designed to help you pinpoint the changes you need to make to build the life you desire. With intentionality & faith, you can build a life you don't need a vacation from. Use this time of reflection to drive what you prioritize each day in your *Forward Planner*.

Reflect on *FAILURE*

What would you do if you weren't afraid to fail?

_____
_____
_____
_____
_____
_____
_____
_____
_____
_____
_____
_____

Would you rather try and fail or never try at all? Which is worse and why?

_____
_____
_____
_____
_____
_____
_____
_____
_____
_____

What failure caused you the most pain and disappointment?

How can the lessons you learned from failure help you move forward?

Reflect on your *FLAWS*

What have you identified as your flaws? Why do you consider these flaws?

_____
_____
_____
_____
_____
_____
_____
_____
_____
_____
_____

Which flaws do you believe are a part of your humanity?

_____
_____
_____
_____
_____
_____
_____
_____

Which flaws do you need to make peace with? Which flaws can you make a plan to improve?

How can your understanding of your flaws help you move forward?

Reflect on your *FEARS*

What is/was your greatest fear? Has it come true?

_____
_____
_____
_____
_____
_____
_____
_____
_____
_____
_____
_____

When faced with fear, how do you respond?

_____
_____
_____
_____
_____
_____
_____
_____
_____

How has fear held you back?

_____

_____

_____

_____

_____

_____

_____

_____

_____

_____

_____

_____

_____

_____

What lessons have you learned about fear that can help you move forward?

_____

_____

_____

_____

_____

_____

_____

_____

_____

_____

_____

_____

_____

_____

Reflect on *FAMILY*

How do you define family?

What has been your experience with family? How have those experiences impacted you?

How much do you depend on those you have defined as family?

How can your family help you move forward?

Reflect on FRIENDS

How do you define genuine friendship?

What do you value most about your friendships?

What has been your experience with friendships?

_____

_____

_____

_____

_____

_____

_____

_____

_____

_____

_____

_____

_____

How can your friends help you move forward?

_____

_____

_____

_____

_____

_____

_____

_____

_____

_____

_____

_____

_____

Reflect on *FORGIVENESS*

Which has more power? Anger or forgiveness? Why?

What do you consider unforgiveable?

Have you forgiven yourself for past mistakes? Why or why not?

How can you use the power of forgiveness to help you move forward?

Reflect on your *FOCUS*

What are your priorities?

What do you need to accomplish these goals?

What distractions make it challenging for you to stay focused?

_____
_____
_____
_____
_____
_____
_____
_____
_____
_____
_____
_____

How will you improve your ability to stay focused on moving forward?

_____
_____
_____
_____
_____
_____
_____
_____
_____
_____
_____
_____

Reflect on your *FAITH*

What has been your experience with faith?

_____
_____
_____
_____
_____
_____
_____
_____
_____
_____
_____

What life circumstances made you cling to your faith harder?

_____
_____
_____
_____
_____
_____
_____
_____

How do you actively grow in your faith?

How can your faith help you move forward?

WHAT DO YOU SEE?

Grab your magazines, glue, scissors, and desired writing utensils! Use this space to create a mini vision board for the life you desire. Don't forget your f- words!

DON'T BE AFRAID to go out *on a limb.*

That's where the fruit is.

MARK TWAIN

How will you "go out on a limb" to move forward this month?

_____
_____
_____
_____
_____
_____
_____
_____
_____
_____

MONTH _____

SUNDAY	MONDAY	TUESDAY	WEDNESDAY
___	___	___	___
___	___	___	___
___	___	___	___
___	___	___	___
___	___	___	___

NOTES

Which F- words will you focus on this month to help you move forward?

focus   fear   failure   forgiveness

faith   family   friends   flaws

THURSDAY	FRIDAY	SATURDAY	WILL DO LIST
——	——	——	
——	——	——	
——	——	——	
——	——	——	
——	——	——	
——	——	——	

WEEK OF _____

SUNDAY

MONDAY

TUESDAY

WEDNESDAY

THURSDAY

FRIDAY

SATURDAY

THIS WEEK'S *WINS*

OPPORTUNITIES FOR IMPROVEMENT

THIS WEEK, I AM GRATEFUL FOR:

WEEK OF _____

SUNDAY

MONDAY

TUESDAY

WEDNESDAY

THURSDAY

FRIDAY

SATURDAY

THIS WEEK'S *WINS*

OPPORTUNITIES FOR IMPROVEMENT

THIS WEEK, I AM GRATEFUL FOR:

WEEK OF _____

SUNDAY

MONDAY

TUESDAY

WEDNESDAY

THURSDAY

FRIDAY

SATURDAY

THIS WEEK'S *WINS*	OPPORTUNITIES FOR IMPROVEMENT

THIS WEEK, I AM GRATEFUL FOR:

WEEK OF _____

SUNDAY

MONDAY

TUESDAY

WEDNESDAY

THURSDAY

FRIDAY

SATURDAY

THIS WEEK'S *WINS*

OPPORTUNITIES FOR IMPROVEMENT

THIS WEEK, I AM GRATEFUL FOR:

WEEK OF _____

SUNDAY

MONDAY

TUESDAY

WEDNESDAY

THURSDAY

FRIDAY

SATURDAY

THIS WEEK'S *WINS*	OPPORTUNITIES FOR IMPROVEMENT

THIS WEEK, I AM GRATEFUL FOR:

END OF MONTH REFLECTIONS

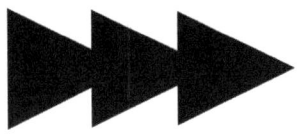

LET'S CELEBRATE! List your top accomplishments.

_____
_____
_____
_____
_____

How will you reward yourself for your accomplishments?

_____
_____

Which F- words helped you move forward this month? (CIRCLE)

focus   fear   failure   forgiveness

faith   family   friends   flaws

What unexpected support or blessing did you receive this month?

_____
_____
_____

List the distractions or obstacles you encountered.

_____
_____
_____
_____
_____

What will you do differently next month to better navigate those distractions or obstacles?

_____
_____
_____
_____
_____

TOP 3 LESSONS LEARNED

How did your faith grow this month?

_____
_____
_____
_____
_____

What will be your top priorities next month?

_____
_____
_____
_____
_____

Family and friendships **ARE TWO OF THE GREATEST FACILITATORS OF HAPPINESS.**

JOHN C. MAXWELL

Do you find happiness with your family and
the friendships you currently have?
Why or why not?

_____
_____
_____
_____
_____
_____
_____
_____
_____
_____
_____

MONTH _____

SUNDAY	MONDAY	TUESDAY	WEDNESDAY
___	___	___	___
___	___	___	___
___	___	___	___
___	___	___	___
___	___	___	___

NOTES
_____
_____
_____
_____

Which F- words will you focus on this month to help you move forward?

focus   fear   failure   forgiveness

faith   family   friends   flaws

THURSDAY	FRIDAY	SATURDAY	WILL DO LIST
___	___	___	
___	___	___	
___	___	___	
___	___	___	
___	___	___	

WEEK OF _____

SUNDAY

MONDAY

TUESDAY

WEDNESDAY

THURSDAY

FRIDAY

SATURDAY

THIS WEEK'S *WINS*	OPPORTUNITIES FOR IMPROVEMENT

THIS WEEK, I AM GRATEFUL FOR:

WEEK OF _____

SUNDAY

MONDAY

TUESDAY

WEDNESDAY

THURSDAY

FRIDAY

SATURDAY

THIS WEEK'S *WINS* | OPPORTUNITIES FOR IMPROVEMENT

THIS WEEK, I AM GRATEFUL FOR:

WEEK OF _____

SUNDAY

MONDAY

TUESDAY

WEDNESDAY

THURSDAY

FRIDAY

SATURDAY

THIS WEEK'S *WINS*	OPPORTUNITIES FOR IMPROVEMENT

THIS WEEK, I AM GRATEFUL FOR:

WEEK OF _____

SUNDAY

MONDAY

TUESDAY

WEDNESDAY

THURSDAY

FRIDAY

SATURDAY

THIS WEEK'S *WINS*

OPPORTUNITIES FOR IMPROVEMENT

THIS WEEK, I AM GRATEFUL FOR:

WEEK OF _____

SUNDAY

MONDAY

TUESDAY

WEDNESDAY

THURSDAY

FRIDAY

SATURDAY

THIS WEEK'S *WINS*	OPPORTUNITIES FOR IMPROVEMENT

THIS WEEK, I AM GRATEFUL FOR:

END OF MONTH REFLECTIONS

LET'S CELEBRATE! List your top accomplishments.

_____
_____
_____
_____

How will you reward yourself for your accomplishments?

_____
_____

Which F- words helped you move forward this month? (CIRCLE)

focus   fear   failure   forgiveness

faith   family   friends   flaws

What unexpected support or blessing did you receive this month?

_____
_____
_____

List the distractions or obstacles you encountered.

_____
_____
_____
_____

What will you do differently next month to better navigate those distractions or obstacles?

TOP 3 LESSONS LEARNED

How did your faith grow this month?

What will be your top priorities next month?

The world will not be convinced of
YOUR FAITH
by the sourness of your face.

UNKNOWN

Ask a close friend to describe your faith walk. Is their description what you thought it would be?

_____
_____
_____
_____
_____
_____
_____
_____
_____
_____

MONTH _____

SUNDAY	MONDAY	TUESDAY	WEDNESDAY
___	___	___	___
___	___	___	___
___	___	___	___
___	___	___	___
___	___	___	___

NOTES
_____
_____
_____
_____
_____

Which F- words will you focus on this month to help you move forward?

focus   fear   failure   forgiveness

faith   family   friends   flaws

THURSDAY	FRIDAY	SATURDAY	WILL DO LIST
___	___	___	
___	___	___	
___	___	___	
___	___	___	
___	___	___	

WEEK OF _____

SUNDAY

MONDAY

TUESDAY

WEDNESDAY

THURSDAY

FRIDAY

SATURDAY

THIS WEEK'S *WINS*	OPPORTUNITIES FOR IMPROVEMENT

THIS WEEK, I AM GRATEFUL FOR:

WEEK OF _____

SUNDAY

MONDAY

TUESDAY

WEDNESDAY

THURSDAY

FRIDAY

SATURDAY

THIS WEEK'S WINS	OPPORTUNITIES FOR IMPROVEMENT

THIS WEEK, I AM GRATEFUL FOR:

WEEK OF _____

SUNDAY

MONDAY

TUESDAY

WEDNESDAY

THURSDAY

FRIDAY

SATURDAY

THIS WEEK'S *WINS*

OPPORTUNITIES FOR IMPROVEMENT

THIS WEEK, I AM GRATEFUL FOR:

WEEK OF _____

SUNDAY

MONDAY

TUESDAY

WEDNESDAY

THURSDAY

FRIDAY

SATURDAY

THIS WEEK'S *WINS*

OPPORTUNITIES FOR IMPROVEMENT

THIS WEEK, I AM GRATEFUL FOR:

WEEK OF _____

SUNDAY

MONDAY

TUESDAY

WEDNESDAY

THURSDAY

FRIDAY

SATURDAY

THIS WEEK'S *WINS*

OPPORTUNITIES FOR IMPROVEMENT

THIS WEEK, I AM GRATEFUL FOR:

END OF MONTH REFLECTIONS

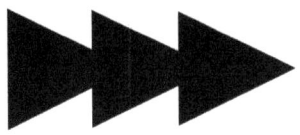

LET'S CELEBRATE! List your top accomplishments.

_____
_____
_____
_____
_____

How will you reward yourself for your accomplishments?

_____
_____

Which F- words helped you move forward this month? (CIRCLE)

focus   fear   failure   forgiveness

faith   family   friends   flaws

What unexpected support or blessing did you receive this month?

_____
_____
_____

List the distractions or obstacles you encountered.

_____
_____
_____
_____
_____

What will you do differently next month to better navigate those distractions or obstacles?

_____
_____
_____
_____
_____

TOP 3 LESSONS LEARNED

How did your faith grow this month?

_____
_____
_____
_____
_____

What will be your top priorities next month?

_____
_____
_____
_____
_____

When you *forgive*, you *heal*.

When you *let go*, you *grow*.

UNKNOWN

What will you release so that you can heal and grow?

_____
_____
_____
_____
_____
_____
_____
_____
_____
_____

MONTH _____

SUNDAY	MONDAY	TUESDAY	WEDNESDAY
___	___	___	___
___	___	___	___
___	___	___	___
___	___	___	___
___	___	___	___

NOTES
_____
_____
_____
_____
_____

Which F- words will you focus on this month to help you move forward?

focus   fear   failure   forgiveness

faith   family   friends   flaws

THURSDAY	FRIDAY	SATURDAY	WILL DO LIST
___	___	___	
___	___	___	
___	___	___	
___	___	___	
___	___	___	

WEEK OF _____

SUNDAY

MONDAY

TUESDAY

WEDNESDAY

THURSDAY

FRIDAY

SATURDAY

THIS WEEK'S *WINS*	OPPORTUNITIES FOR IMPROVEMENT

THIS WEEK, I AM GRATEFUL FOR:

WEEK OF _____

SUNDAY

MONDAY

TUESDAY

WEDNESDAY

THURSDAY

FRIDAY

SATURDAY

THIS WEEK'S *WINS*

OPPORTUNITIES FOR IMPROVEMENT

THIS WEEK, I AM GRATEFUL FOR:

WEEK OF _____

SUNDAY

MONDAY

TUESDAY

WEDNESDAY

THURSDAY

FRIDAY

SATURDAY

THIS WEEK'S *WINS*	OPPORTUNITIES FOR IMPROVEMENT

THIS WEEK, I AM GRATEFUL FOR:

WEEK OF _____

SUNDAY

MONDAY

TUESDAY

WEDNESDAY

THURSDAY

FRIDAY

SATURDAY

THIS WEEK'S *WINS*

OPPORTUNITIES FOR IMPROVEMENT

THIS WEEK, I AM GRATEFUL FOR:

WEEK OF _____

SUNDAY

MONDAY

TUESDAY

WEDNESDAY

THURSDAY

FRIDAY

SATURDAY

THIS WEEK'S *WINS*	OPPORTUNITIES FOR IMPROVEMENT

THIS WEEK, I AM GRATEFUL FOR:

END OF MONTH REFLECTIONS

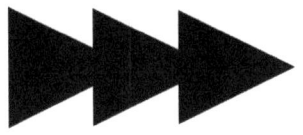

LET'S CELEBRATE! List your top accomplishments.

_____
_____
_____
_____
_____

How will you reward yourself for your accomplishments?

_____
_____

Which F- words helped you move forward this month? (CIRCLE)

focus   fear   failure   forgiveness

faith   family   friends   flaws

What unexpected support or blessing did you receive this month?

_____
_____
_____

List the distractions or obstacles you encountered.

_____
_____
_____
_____
_____

What will you do differently next month to better navigate those distractions or obstacles?

TOP 3 LESSONS LEARNED

How did your faith grow this month?

What will be your top priorities next month?

A REAL FRIEND
never gets in your way
unless
you
happen
to
be
on
the
way
down
…

ARNOLD GLASOW

Which friend can you count on to pull you out of a low place? How did you learn they were capable of uplifting you?

___

MONTH _____

SUNDAY	MONDAY	TUESDAY	WEDNESDAY
___	___	___	___
___	___	___	___
___	___	___	___
___	___	___	___
___	___	___	___
___	___	___	___

NOTES
_____
_____
_____
_____

Which F- words will you focus on this month to help you move forward?

focus   fear   failure   forgiveness

faith   family   friends   flaws

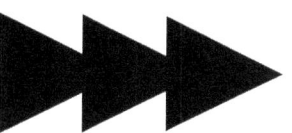

THURSDAY	FRIDAY	SATURDAY	WILL DO LIST
___	___	___	
___	___	___	
___	___	___	
___	___	___	
___	___	___	
___	___	___	

WEEK OF _____

SUNDAY

MONDAY

TUESDAY

WEDNESDAY

THURSDAY

FRIDAY

SATURDAY

THIS WEEK'S *WINS*	OPPORTUNITIES FOR IMPROVEMENT

THIS WEEK, I AM GRATEFUL FOR:

WEEK OF _____

SUNDAY

MONDAY

TUESDAY

WEDNESDAY

THURSDAY

FRIDAY

SATURDAY

THIS WEEK'S *WINS*

OPPORTUNITIES FOR IMPROVEMENT

THIS WEEK, I AM GRATEFUL FOR:

WEEK OF _____

SUNDAY

MONDAY

TUESDAY

WEDNESDAY

THURSDAY

FRIDAY

SATURDAY

THIS WEEK'S *WINS*

OPPORTUNITIES FOR IMPROVEMENT

THIS WEEK, I AM GRATEFUL FOR:

WEEK OF _____

SUNDAY

MONDAY

TUESDAY

WEDNESDAY

THURSDAY

FRIDAY

SATURDAY

THIS WEEK'S *WINS*	OPPORTUNITIES FOR IMPROVEMENT

THIS WEEK, I AM GRATEFUL FOR:

WEEK OF _____

SUNDAY

MONDAY

TUESDAY

WEDNESDAY

THURSDAY

FRIDAY

SATURDAY

THIS WEEK'S *WINS*

OPPORTUNITIES FOR IMPROVEMENT

THIS WEEK, I AM GRATEFUL FOR:

END OF MONTH REFLECTIONS

LET'S CELEBRATE! List your top accomplishments.

_____
_____
_____
_____
_____

How will you reward yourself for your accomplishments?

_____
_____

Which F- words helped you move forward this month? (CIRCLE)

focus   fear   failure   forgiveness

faith   family   friends   flaws

What unexpected support or blessing did you receive this month?

_____
_____
_____

List the distractions or obstacles you encountered.

_____
_____
_____
_____
_____

What will you do differently next month to better navigate those distractions or obstacles?

___

TOP 3 LESSONS LEARNED

☐ ☐ ☐

How did your faith grow this month?

___

What will be your top priorities next month?

___

People don't accidentally
stumble
into failure.

They *think* their way into it.

KAMAL RAVIKANT

What limiting beliefs are causing you to fail in your personal or career goals? Why?

_____
_____
_____
_____
_____
_____
_____
_____
_____
_____

MONTH _____

SUNDAY	MONDAY	TUESDAY	WEDNESDAY
___	___	___	___
___	___	___	___
___	___	___	___
___	___	___	___
___	___	___	___

NOTES _____
_____
_____
_____
_____

Which F- words will you focus on this month to help you move forward?

focus   fear   failure   forgiveness

faith   family   friends   flaws

THURSDAY	FRIDAY	SATURDAY	WILL DO LIST
___	___	___	
___	___	___	
___	___	___	
___	___	___	
___	___	___	

WEEK OF _____

SUNDAY

MONDAY

TUESDAY

WEDNESDAY

THURSDAY

FRIDAY

SATURDAY

THIS WEEK'S *WINS*

OPPORTUNITIES FOR IMPROVEMENT

THIS WEEK, I AM GRATEFUL FOR:

WEEK OF _____

SUNDAY

MONDAY

TUESDAY

WEDNESDAY

THURSDAY

FRIDAY

SATURDAY

THIS WEEK'S *WINS*

OPPORTUNITIES FOR IMPROVEMENT

THIS WEEK, I AM GRATEFUL FOR:

WEEK OF _____

SUNDAY

MONDAY

TUESDAY

WEDNESDAY

THURSDAY

FRIDAY

SATURDAY

THIS WEEK'S *WINS*	OPPORTUNITIES FOR IMPROVEMENT

THIS WEEK, I AM GRATEFUL FOR:

WEEK OF _____

SUNDAY

MONDAY

TUESDAY

WEDNESDAY

THURSDAY

FRIDAY

SATURDAY

THIS WEEK'S *WINS*	OPPORTUNITIES FOR IMPROVEMENT

THIS WEEK, I AM GRATEFUL FOR:

WEEK OF _____

SUNDAY

MONDAY

TUESDAY

WEDNESDAY

THURSDAY

FRIDAY

SATURDAY

THIS WEEK'S *WINS*	OPPORTUNITIES FOR IMPROVEMENT

THIS WEEK, I AM GRATEFUL FOR:

END OF MONTH REFLECTIONS

LET'S CELEBRATE! List your top accomplishments.

_____
_____
_____
_____
_____

How will you reward yourself for your accomplishments?

_____
_____

Which F- words helped you move forward this month? (CIRCLE)

focus   fear   failure   forgiveness

faith   family   friends   flaws

What unexpected support or blessing did you receive this month?

_____
_____
_____

List the distractions or obstacles you encountered.

_____
_____
_____
_____
_____

What will you do differently next month to better navigate those distractions or obstacles?

_____
_____
_____
_____
_____

TOP 3 LESSONS LEARNED

How did your faith grow this month?

_____
_____
_____
_____
_____

What will be your top priorities next month?

_____
_____
_____
_____
_____

Let your eyes look directly forward, and your gaze be straight before you.

PROVERBS 4:25

Where is your gaze? Is it where it should be? What adjustments are necessary for your focus?

_____
_____
_____
_____
_____
_____
_____
_____
_____
_____

MONTH _____

SUNDAY	MONDAY	TUESDAY	WEDNESDAY
___	___	___	___
___	___	___	___
___	___	___	___
___	___	___	___
___	___	___	___

NOTES _____
_____
_____
_____
_____

Which F- words will you focus on this month to help you move forward?

focus   fear   failure   forgiveness

faith   family   friends   flaws

THURSDAY	FRIDAY	SATURDAY	WILL DO LIST
___	___	___	
___	___	___	
___	___	___	
___	___	___	

WEEK OF ⎯⎯⎯⎯⎯⎯⎯⎯⎯⎯⎯⎯⎯⎯⎯⎯⎯⎯

SUNDAY

MONDAY

TUESDAY

WEDNESDAY

THURSDAY

FRIDAY

SATURDAY

THIS WEEK'S *WINS*

OPPORTUNITIES FOR IMPROVEMENT

THIS WEEK, I AM GRATEFUL FOR:

WEEK OF _____

SUNDAY

MONDAY

TUESDAY

WEDNESDAY

THURSDAY

FRIDAY

SATURDAY

THIS WEEK'S *WINS*	OPPORTUNITIES FOR IMPROVEMENT

THIS WEEK, I AM GRATEFUL FOR:

WEEK OF _____

SUNDAY

MONDAY

TUESDAY

WEDNESDAY

THURSDAY

FRIDAY

SATURDAY

THIS WEEK'S *WINS*

OPPORTUNITIES FOR IMPROVEMENT

THIS WEEK, I AM GRATEFUL FOR:

WEEK OF _____

SUNDAY

MONDAY

TUESDAY

WEDNESDAY

THURSDAY

FRIDAY

SATURDAY

THIS WEEK'S *WINS*

OPPORTUNITIES FOR IMPROVEMENT

THIS WEEK, I AM GRATEFUL FOR:

WEEK OF _____

SUNDAY

MONDAY

TUESDAY

WEDNESDAY

THURSDAY

FRIDAY

SATURDAY

THIS WEEK'S *WINS*	OPPORTUNITIES FOR IMPROVEMENT

THIS WEEK, I AM GRATEFUL FOR:

END OF MONTH REFLECTIONS

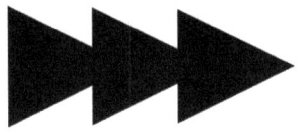

LET'S CELEBRATE! List your top accomplishments.

_____
_____
_____
_____
_____

How will you reward yourself for your accomplishments?

_____
_____

Which F- words helped you move forward this month? (CIRCLE)

focus   fear   failure   forgiveness

faith   family   friends   flaws

What unexpected support or blessing did you receive this month?

_____
_____
_____

List the distractions or obstacles you encountered.

_____
_____
_____
_____
_____

What will you do differently next month to better navigate those distractions or obstacles?

___

TOP 3 LESSONS LEARNED

How did your faith grow this month?

___

What will be your top priorities next month?

___

As long as we are persistent in our pursuit of our deepest destiny, we will continue to grow.

We cannot choose the day or time when we will fully bloom. It happens in its own time.

DENIS WAITLEY

What frustrations do you face as you strive to strengthen your weaknesses?

_____
_____
_____
_____
_____
_____
_____
_____
_____
_____

MONTH _____

SUNDAY	MONDAY	TUESDAY	WEDNESDAY
___	___	___	___
___	___	___	___
___	___	___	___
___	___	___	___
___	___	___	___

NOTES _____
_____
_____
_____
_____

Which F- words will you focus on this month to help you move forward?

focus   fear   failure   forgiveness

faith   family   friends   flaws

THURSDAY	FRIDAY	SATURDAY	WILL DO LIST
___	___	___	
___	___	___	
___	___	___	
___	___	___	

WEEK OF _____

SUNDAY

MONDAY

TUESDAY

WEDNESDAY

THURSDAY

FRIDAY

SATURDAY

THIS WEEK'S *WINS*

OPPORTUNITIES FOR IMPROVEMENT

THIS WEEK, I AM GRATEFUL FOR:

WEEK OF _____

SUNDAY

MONDAY

TUESDAY

WEDNESDAY

THURSDAY

FRIDAY

SATURDAY

THIS WEEK'S *WINS*	OPPORTUNITIES FOR IMPROVEMENT

THIS WEEK, I AM GRATEFUL FOR:

WEEK OF _____

SUNDAY

MONDAY

TUESDAY

WEDNESDAY

THURSDAY

FRIDAY

SATURDAY

THIS WEEK'S *WINS*	OPPORTUNITIES FOR IMPROVEMENT

THIS WEEK, I AM GRATEFUL FOR:

WEEK OF _____

SUNDAY

MONDAY

TUESDAY

WEDNESDAY

THURSDAY

FRIDAY

SATURDAY

THIS WEEK'S *WINS*

OPPORTUNITIES FOR IMPROVEMENT

THIS WEEK, I AM GRATEFUL FOR:

WEEK OF _____

SUNDAY

MONDAY

TUESDAY

WEDNESDAY

THURSDAY

FRIDAY

SATURDAY

THIS WEEK'S *WINS*

OPPORTUNITIES FOR IMPROVEMENT

THIS WEEK, I AM GRATEFUL FOR:

END OF MONTH REFLECTIONS

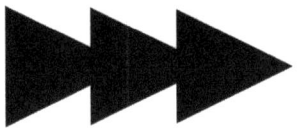

LET'S CELEBRATE! List your top accomplishments.

_____
_____
_____
_____
_____

How will you reward yourself for your accomplishments?

_____
_____

Which F- words helped you move forward this month? (CIRCLE)

focus   fear   failure   forgiveness

faith   family   friends   flaws

What unexpected support or blessing did you receive this month?

_____
_____
_____

List the distractions or obstacles you encountered.

_____
_____
_____
_____
_____

What will you do differently next month to better navigate those distractions or obstacles?

___

TOP 3 LESSONS LEARNED

How did your faith grow this month?

___

What will be your top priorities next month?

___

If everyone is moving forward
TOGETHER
then success takes care of
itself.

HENRY FORD

Do you have a team to support you as you pursue your goals? How do you strive to move forward together?

_____
_____
_____
_____
_____
_____
_____
_____
_____

MONTH _____

SUNDAY	MONDAY	TUESDAY	WEDNESDAY
___	___	___	___
___	___	___	___
___	___	___	___
___	___	___	___
___	___	___	___

NOTES
_____
_____
_____
_____
_____

Which F- words will you focus on this month to help you move forward?

focus   fear   failure   forgiveness

faith   family   friends   flaws

THURSDAY	FRIDAY	SATURDAY	WILL DO LIST
___	___	___	
___	___	___	
___	___	___	
___	___	___	
___	___	___	
___	___	___	

WEEK OF _____

SUNDAY

MONDAY

TUESDAY

WEDNESDAY

THURSDAY

FRIDAY

SATURDAY

THIS WEEK'S *WINS*

OPPORTUNITIES FOR IMPROVEMENT

THIS WEEK, I AM GRATEFUL FOR:

WEEK OF _____

SUNDAY

MONDAY

TUESDAY

WEDNESDAY

THURSDAY

FRIDAY

SATURDAY

THIS WEEK'S *WINS*

OPPORTUNITIES FOR IMPROVEMENT

THIS WEEK, I AM GRATEFUL FOR:

WEEK OF _____

SUNDAY

MONDAY

TUESDAY

WEDNESDAY

THURSDAY

FRIDAY

SATURDAY

THIS WEEK'S *WINS*

OPPORTUNITIES FOR IMPROVEMENT

THIS WEEK, I AM GRATEFUL FOR:

WEEK OF _____

SUNDAY

MONDAY

TUESDAY

WEDNESDAY

THURSDAY

FRIDAY

SATURDAY

THIS WEEK'S *WINS*

OPPORTUNITIES FOR IMPROVEMENT

THIS WEEK, I AM GRATEFUL FOR:

WEEK OF _____

SUNDAY

MONDAY

TUESDAY

WEDNESDAY

THURSDAY

FRIDAY

SATURDAY

THIS WEEK'S *WINS*

OPPORTUNITIES FOR IMPROVEMENT

THIS WEEK, I AM GRATEFUL FOR:

END OF MONTH REFLECTIONS

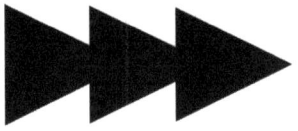

LET'S CELEBRATE! List your top accomplishments.

_____
_____
_____
_____
_____

How will you reward yourself for your accomplishments?

_____
_____

Which F- words helped you move forward this month? (CIRCLE)

focus   fear   failure   forgiveness

faith   family   friends   flaws

What unexpected support or blessing did you receive this month?

_____
_____
_____

List the distractions or obstacles you encountered.

_____
_____
_____
_____
_____

What will you do differently next month to better navigate those distractions or obstacles?

_____
_____
_____
_____

TOP 3 LESSONS LEARNED

How did your faith grow this month?

_____
_____
_____
_____

What will be your top priorities next month?

_____
_____
_____
_____

For we walk by
FAITH,
NOT BY SIGHT...

2 CORINTHIANS 5:7

What is the difference between what you see and what you believe?

_____
_____
_____
_____
_____
_____
_____
_____
_____
_____
_____

MONTH _____

SUNDAY	MONDAY	TUESDAY	WEDNESDAY
__	__	__	__
__	__	__	__
__	__	__	__
__	__	__	__
__	__	__	__
__	__	__	__

NOTES
_____
_____
_____
_____
_____

Which F- words will you focus on this month to help you move forward?

focus   fear   failure   forgiveness

faith   family   friends   flaws

THURSDAY	FRIDAY	SATURDAY	WILL DO LIST
___	___	___	
___	___	___	
___	___	___	
___	___	___	
___	___	___	

WEEK OF _____

SUNDAY

MONDAY

TUESDAY

WEDNESDAY

THURSDAY

FRIDAY

SATURDAY

THIS WEEK'S *WINS*

OPPORTUNITIES FOR IMPROVEMENT

THIS WEEK, I AM GRATEFUL FOR:

WEEK OF _____

SUNDAY

MONDAY

TUESDAY

WEDNESDAY

THURSDAY

FRIDAY

SATURDAY

THIS WEEK'S *WINS*

OPPORTUNITIES FOR IMPROVEMENT

THIS WEEK, I AM GRATEFUL FOR:

WEEK OF _____

SUNDAY

MONDAY

TUESDAY

WEDNESDAY

THURSDAY

FRIDAY

SATURDAY

THIS WEEK'S *WINS*

OPPORTUNITIES FOR IMPROVEMENT

THIS WEEK, I AM GRATEFUL FOR:

WEEK OF _____

SUNDAY

MONDAY

TUESDAY

WEDNESDAY

THURSDAY

FRIDAY

SATURDAY

THIS WEEK'S *WINS*	OPPORTUNITIES FOR IMPROVEMENT

THIS WEEK, I AM GRATEFUL FOR:

WEEK OF _____

SUNDAY

MONDAY

TUESDAY

WEDNESDAY

THURSDAY

FRIDAY

SATURDAY

THIS WEEK'S *WINS*	OPPORTUNITIES FOR IMPROVEMENT

THIS WEEK, I AM GRATEFUL FOR:

END OF MONTH REFLECTIONS

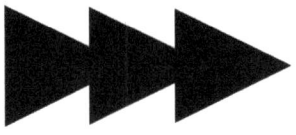

LET'S CELEBRATE! List your top accomplishments.

_____
_____
_____
_____
_____

How will you reward yourself for your accomplishments?

_____
_____

Which F- words helped you move forward this month? (CIRCLE)

focus   fear   failure   forgiveness

faith   family   friends   flaws

What unexpected support or blessing did you receive this month?

_____
_____
_____

List the distractions or obstacles you encountered.

_____
_____
_____
_____
_____

What will you do differently next month to better navigate those distractions or obstacles?

_____
_____
_____
_____
_____

TOP 3 LESSONS LEARNED

How did your faith grow this month?

_____
_____
_____
_____
_____

What will be your top priorities next month?

_____
_____
_____
_____
_____

Both FAITH AND FEAR *sail* into the harbor of your mind, *but only faith should be allowed to anchor.*

BEAR GRYLLS

What have you allowed to anchor in the harbor of your mind? Why?

_____
_____
_____
_____
_____
_____
_____
_____
_____

MONTH _____

SUNDAY	MONDAY	TUESDAY	WEDNESDAY
__	__	__	__
__	__	__	__
__	__	__	__
__	__	__	__
__	__	__	__

NOTES

Which F- words will you focus on this month to help you move forward?

focus   fear   failure   forgiveness

faith   family   friends   flaws

THURSDAY	FRIDAY	SATURDAY	WILL DO LIST
___	___	___	
___	___	___	
___	___	___	
___	___	___	
___	___	___	

WEEK OF _____

SUNDAY

MONDAY

TUESDAY

WEDNESDAY

THURSDAY

FRIDAY

SATURDAY

THIS WEEK'S *WINS*

OPPORTUNITIES FOR IMPROVEMENT

THIS WEEK, I AM GRATEFUL FOR:

WEEK OF _____

SUNDAY

MONDAY

TUESDAY

WEDNESDAY

THURSDAY

FRIDAY

SATURDAY

THIS WEEK'S *WINS*

OPPORTUNITIES FOR IMPROVEMENT

THIS WEEK, I AM GRATEFUL FOR:

WEEK OF _____

SUNDAY

MONDAY

TUESDAY

WEDNESDAY

THURSDAY

FRIDAY

SATURDAY

THIS WEEK'S *WINS*	OPPORTUNITIES FOR IMPROVEMENT

THIS WEEK, I AM GRATEFUL FOR:

WEEK OF _____

SUNDAY

MONDAY

TUESDAY

WEDNESDAY

THURSDAY

FRIDAY

SATURDAY

THIS WEEK'S *WINS*

OPPORTUNITIES FOR IMPROVEMENT

THIS WEEK, I AM GRATEFUL FOR:

WEEK OF _____

SUNDAY

MONDAY

TUESDAY

WEDNESDAY

THURSDAY

FRIDAY

SATURDAY

THIS WEEK'S *WINS*

OPPORTUNITIES FOR IMPROVEMENT

THIS WEEK, I AM GRATEFUL FOR:

END OF MONTH REFLECTIONS

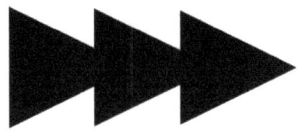

LET'S CELEBRATE! List your top accomplishments.

_____
_____
_____
_____

How will you reward yourself for your accomplishments?

_____
_____

Which F- words helped you move forward this month? (CIRCLE)

focus   fear   failure   forgiveness

faith   family   friends   flaws

What unexpected support or blessing did you receive this month?

_____
_____
_____

List the distractions or obstacles you encountered.

_____
_____
_____
_____

What will you do differently next month to better navigate those distractions or obstacles?

_____
_____
_____
_____

TOP 3 LESSONS LEARNED

How did your faith grow this month?

_____
_____
_____
_____

What will be your top priorities or focuses next month?

_____
_____
_____
_____

No matter what happens, or how bad it seems today, life does go on, and it will be better tomorrow.

MAYA ANGELOU

How will your *later on* be better than your *right now*? What adjustments will you make to ensure improvement is inevitable?

_____
_____
_____
_____
_____
_____
_____
_____
_____
_____

MONTH _____

SUNDAY	MONDAY	TUESDAY	WEDNESDAY
__	__	__	__
__	__	__	__
__	__	__	__
__	__	__	__
__	__	__	__
__	__	__	__

NOTES _____
_____
_____
_____
_____

Which F- words will you focus on this month to help you move forward?

focus   fear   failure   forgiveness

faith   family   friends   flaws

THURSDAY	FRIDAY	SATURDAY	WILL DO LIST
___	___	___	
___	___	___	
___	___	___	
___	___	___	

WEEK OF _____

SUNDAY

MONDAY

TUESDAY

WEDNESDAY

THURSDAY

FRIDAY

SATURDAY

THIS WEEK'S *WINS*	OPPORTUNITIES FOR IMPROVEMENT

THIS WEEK, I AM GRATEFUL FOR:

WEEK OF _____

SUNDAY

MONDAY

TUESDAY

WEDNESDAY

THURSDAY

FRIDAY

SATURDAY

THIS WEEK'S *WINS*

OPPORTUNITIES FOR IMPROVEMENT

THIS WEEK, I AM GRATEFUL FOR:

WEEK OF _____

SUNDAY

MONDAY

TUESDAY

WEDNESDAY

THURSDAY

FRIDAY

SATURDAY

THIS WEEK'S *WINS*

OPPORTUNITIES FOR IMPROVEMENT

THIS WEEK, I AM GRATEFUL FOR:

WEEK OF _____

SUNDAY

MONDAY

TUESDAY

WEDNESDAY

THURSDAY

FRIDAY

SATURDAY

THIS WEEK'S *WINS*

OPPORTUNITIES FOR IMPROVEMENT

THIS WEEK, I AM GRATEFUL FOR:

WEEK OF _____

SUNDAY

MONDAY

TUESDAY

WEDNESDAY

THURSDAY

FRIDAY

SATURDAY

THIS WEEK'S *WINS*

OPPORTUNITIES FOR IMPROVEMENT

THIS WEEK, I AM GRATEFUL FOR:

END OF MONTH REFLECTIONS

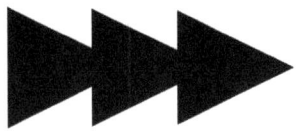

LET'S CELEBRATE! List your top accomplishments.

_____
_____
_____
_____
_____

How will you reward yourself for your accomplishments?

_____
_____

Which F- words helped you move forward this month? (CIRCLE)

focus   fear   failure   forgiveness

faith   family   friends   flaws

What unexpected support or blessing did you receive this month?

_____
_____
_____

List the distractions or obstacles you encountered.

_____
_____
_____
_____
_____

What will you do differently next month to better navigate those distractions or obstacles?

TOP 3 LESSONS LEARNED

How did your faith grow this month?

What will be your top priorities next month?

NOTES

www.ingramcontent.com/pod-product-compliance
Lightning Source LLC
Chambersburg PA
CBHW061351010526
44107CB00011B/907